Less Than a Sack of Weed

Principles for the Hood

Cliff Green

Dedication

I write this with love to my family and friends, who saw the vision and ensured that I never wavered from it!

To the woman who believed in, supported, and continually pushed me to be the best man I could be, forever isn't long enough! If I was only wise enough to understand.

Preface

Less Than a Sack of Weed is a culmination of writings originally posted on **25BlackAndAlive.com**. The initial title was *This Book Cost Less Than a Sack of Weed* until my beautiful sister, Stephanie, convinced me to shorten it *to Less Than a Sack of Weed*.

I wanted a title that would catch your eye and make you ask yourself, "What does that mean?" Not that I am against smoking weed, but every day, people make decisions that do not benefit them in the long run.

For instance, a gram of loud (weed), widely known as a sack, costs a dub ($20). The highs and the effects of weed are temporary. You will get two to three hours of sensation at best.

This book and many others cost well below a sack of weed. The benefits and highs you will get from reading this book will last a lifetime. You can choose to buy a gram, or you can choose to buy a book. Decisions. Decisions.

I intend to help you make the best decisions as often as possible. Everything you do and accomplish in life boils down to your choices.

As for who I am and why writing this book was so important, I grew up in a little hood called Wilkinsburg, and I witnessed firsthand how one wrong decision could cripple an entire family. I still live in a hood by choice, though I can live elsewhere. I don't want to be so far removed from my beloved community and unable to relate to reality.

I have survived and overcome the obstacles placed before me. I have learned a few lessons during my short time here on earth, and I am working hard to ensure that the next generation learns those lessons in half the time.

If your goal is to better your life and the lives of the people around you, this book **is** for you. The stories and principles within will help put the power in your hands. Once you have conquered the world and it's in your palm, you can pass the rock to the next man.

This is a snippet of the thought-provoking text within this book:

Consequences are the direct result of doing the opposite of what you knew you were supposed to do.

You can choose to *Go Hard or Die Easy,* but you will learn more about that as you read along.

With much love, I bring you *Less Than a Sack of Weed!*

Contents

Street Credit is Dead

I'm from the hood, and it's the same story everywhere. Young men want to earn their stripes. They want people to know that they're a man.

The hood breeds this mentality that gangbanging, selling drugs, or having sex with many women is the way. Many of our young men want their claim to fame from the streets. They want to earn street credit.

Walk with me through the streets of D.C.

I remember this one day: I passed by this man and said, "What up, brother?" He responded, "What's up, Black man?"

His response intrigued me, so I stopped and conversed with him.

I told him I appreciated him for acknowledging me, especially how he did. I explained to him that people barely look me in the eye when I walk through the streets and do everything possible to avoid speaking to me as if I were their enemy.

We talked for a few minutes, agreeing that it was wild that no one liked to speak anymore and that we wished for simpler days when respect and common courtesy were common. Then, he handed me his card, and I continued on my way.

Around eight o'clock that evening, I went to the library to study. Afterward, I went to the grocery store to grab a few things. The walk from the grocery store to my house was about fifteen minutes long. I carried fifteen to twenty pounds of groceries in each arm and had a twenty-five-pound book bag on my back.

I came upon five or six young males chilling by an elementary school gate on my way home. They all appeared to be in their teens, so I thought nothing of it, but I guess the lady in front of me knew better. She walked in the street to avoid them. I stayed on the sidewalk, and as I got twenty-five to thirty feet past them, I heard a clump and felt something slide down the side of my shirt. I turned around and saw a nice-sized rock on the ground.

Another young bull was leaning on a gate closer to where I was, watching the whole thing.

He said, "Oooh, they're wildin'!"

I said, "Yeah, they are, but I could've sworn we were all brothers living in the same struggle! But that's cool!"

Young Bull said, "I respect that!"

I nodded my head at him, turned around, and kept walking.

Ten minutes later, the pain finally hit me when I arrived at my house. It wasn't a physical pain. It was more of a spiritual and mental pain. I am not comparing myself to Yahshuah (Jesus), but His story immediately popped into my head.

No matter how right you may be, there will always be opposition. The Most High then reaffirmed the truths within Psalms 91:10, "No harm shall befall you; No disaster shall come near your tent." Think about that. One of them threw a rock at my back. It could've struck me anywhere and severely hurt me, but it hit my bookbag.

I sat, cried, and prayed to the Most High, asking him why *I cared so much. Why do I put myself through the torment? Why keep working so hard to help people, only to receive pain?* I was pained and tormented by our hatred for one another.

The streets breed hate and fear, which will keep us divided forever. Street credit has messed up many of our young men's priorities. To my young men reading this, a man's priority is to think before acting.

I could've had a gun on my hip, turned around, and sprayed at everyone. At that moment, that young man wasn't thinking about or prioritizing his future. He thought of the points (Street Credit) he would have earned with his boys. How many points would he have earned if I did turn around and take his or one of his friends' lives?

Companies are buying all the land and forcing people out of their homes. Gentrification is happening across America. Men with priorities know all about it and do what they can to protect their communities. Boys try to obtain street credit by throwing rocks at people they don't know.

As I discussed with the man earlier, *Am I your enemy?*

To make the story worse, this incident happened at Malcolm X Elementary. It's time to reevaluate what we see as cool. Being what you think is disrespectful isn't disrespectful to that person but to yourself and every ancestor who came before you.

Street credit will get you nothing positive in life. It only gives you three options to choose from:

1. a six by eight cell,
2. six feet under or
3. probation.

Street credit leaves you constantly looking over your shoulder every time you step foot outside.

Have you ever seen a man buy a house with street credit? Have you ever seen a man buy a car with street credit? Of course, some guys have cars and maybe a home, but is it in their name? Try to leave the country while on probation and see what happens.

Street Credit should be called "Burial Credit" because death is the only thing it earns. Let's make earning real credit a priority. Real credit will change the quality of your life and circumstances.

It's time to get our priorities in order. Street Credit doesn't even make the list. Street Credit is dead. Let's bury it!

Somebody's Watching

In this age of Facebook, Twitter, and Instagram, everyone wants you to subscribe to or follow them. My question to everyone is, *what are you doing that is so special that I, or anyone else, should tag along for the ride?*

Are you productive and helping to build meaning in peoples' lives? Or do you want everyone to know where you are and what possessions you have? No matter what you do, whether posting pictures on the web or simply walking down the street, know that **somebody's watching**!

In D.C., the Metro takes you in four directions: northeast, northwest, southeast, and southwest. I live in Southeast D.C., Congress Heights, to be exact. The Congress Heights Metro station has five escalators and one set of stairs, totaling one hundred and eighteen steps. I usually take the steps instead of the escalator. I also like to run these steps for a good workout.

One day, as I was leaving the station and climbing the steps as usual, I made it one flight up before I heard a lady say to her son, "Oh, so you're going to take the steps, too?"

I looked back, and to my surprise, I saw a young bull running up the steps behind me. He was watching me and wanted to hit the steps himself. In my mind, I thought, *Word!*

I continued my climb while constantly shouting words of encouragement to him. As we arrived at the top, he was out of breath, huffing and puffing. I shook his hand and introduced myself to him as Mr. Cliff. I asked him his name, and he told me it was Machiavelli. Then, I asked him if he noticed how hard work and dedication led him to the top (a life metaphor/lesson).

He continued to huff and puff while looking like he had just accomplished a goal he had set out years ago. He watched me do something he may have wanted to do for years, but other people may have discouraged him. I waited for his mother to get the top and then told her how strong her son was.

This encounter may have influenced Machiavelli to take the steps daily for the rest of his life. A choice that could make him stronger than his peers, and if he chooses to play a sport, it will help him run, think, and maneuver faster than his counterparts.

That choice may increase his health and, in doing so, increase his lifespan. The choice he made that day will surely affect his tomorrow.

This kid unknowingly inspired me to keep doing what I was doing. He didn't know that I walked and ran those steps not solely for personal benefit but also to encourage others to do the same. He didn't know that he gave me hope for the future, and if I continue to be positive, that positivity will eventually spread to someone else. When you see a ray of light in a world full of darkness, it pushes you forward with the hope that a better day will come.

I don't write this hoping that you will become a follower of mine. I pray that you become a leader. I pray that I have planted a seed of inspiration and courage within you to dare to be different. I mean to really be different. Try being untrendy. Go in the opposite direction of the crowd. It won't be easy to get to the other side while weaving through people pushing and pulling you in every different direction.

You will be in your own lane when you get to the other side. Just know that somebody saw you going in the opposite direction of the crowd. The people who see you and have the courage not to follow the herd will turn around and go on their own path. That's what real leaders do, and you have just become one.

Again, I ask, *If I, or anyone else, was watching you, where would you be leading us?*

Blessings Disguised as a Curse

In my late teens, I had acne. I saw acne as a curse that was bent on destroying my life. I tried everything on the market, from over-the-counter drugs and face washes to prescriptions to get rid of my acne. My acne took a turn for the worse when I decided to see a dermatologist, who prescribed me a drug that was a notch under Accutane. I can't recall the exact name, but boy, oh boy! My face broke out horribly.

This breakout happened the summer before my sophomore year in college. I entered that year of school hating myself. I thought I was the ugliest person around. I felt cursed. I didn't know why or how this was happening to me. I remember looking in the mirror at both sides of my face, using a handheld mirror for a side view.

I was in so much anguish that thoughts of death and suicide crossed my mind for some time. Death seemed to be a better option than going through life with this torment. I didn't know how I could go on. I felt embarrassed to be in public. I didn't want to go to school.

While in school, I used the internet for schoolwork and personal use. I searched the internet for anything and everything to get rid of acne.

The cure finally came to me. I needed to flush my system and change my eating habits. Our American diets and lifestyles are toxic. The foods we eat are not natural to our bodies. They only build up toxins within them.

The toxins came out of me through my skin, which caused acne. These toxins may affect you in different ways. For you, it could be high blood pressure, obesity, diabetes, eczema, bad breath, cancer, and a list of other illnesses.

Finally, after some years, my curse turned into a blessing. Finding the cure and implementing the necessary steps to rid myself of acne led to other positive things in my life. For instance, I feel and look better than I ever have. Plus, my energy levels are through the roof. And since I do not eat junk food like I used to, I have excess money in my pocket.

When you research enough, you may discover other pieces of information. The more I learned, the clearer my mind became. I was led to real history instead of a one-sided view, which school had taught me.

Now, I can see through this world full of lies and deception. I couldn't tell you if I would be the man I am today if I didn't have acne. I probably would be the same average guy, only worried about money, sex, cars, and whatever other nonsense the world tells us to worry about.

I don't know if I would still prioritize service to others had I not gotten acne. The curse of acne became a blessing of wisdom, knowledge, and understanding, which I intend to spread to everyone willing to listen to or read this book.

It sounds cliché, but all negatives can be turned into positives. Know that everything that happens is for a reason. The old saying, "God will never give you more than you can handle!" is true. It would be best to display patience and faith that the Most High has a plan for you.

The Bible speaks about the vigilant student you must be in this lifetime.

Ask, and it will be given to you; seek, and you will find; knock, and the door will be opened for you. For everyone who asks receives; the one who seeks finds; and to the one who knocks, the door will be opened.
(Matthew 7:7-8)

Know that the answers are out there. More importantly, the answers are within you. Take the time to study for yourself. The answers and blessings will come to you, and I promise the result will be a better you.

It took me years to realize that my curse was a blessing in disguise. My prayer is that this short story of my life will bring you your blessings in half the time.

Don't be a Sitting Duck

I am not boasting or bragging, but I am highly athletic. I am strong, fast, and agile. Health and wellness are a priority in my life. My goal is to get you there if you're not already.

Let's pretend that I was a devil in the hood who loved to rob, steal, kill, and hurt people. You run into me, a devil, and tonight, I'm walking around looking for my next come-up. Here you are, walking through a backstreet or alley because it's a quicker route to get home. Suddenly, you hear a shot go off and feel a sharp, swift wind blaze on your face. You know someone is coming at you.

Your only option is to run, but you can't take off because you're *duck walking* due to your pants sagging. Your pants are falling; you have one hand on your waist and the other swinging normally. You're trying to run away, but you get caught. I end up robbing you, severely hurting you, or taking your life. A situation you could've escaped if your pants weren't in the way. Sagging turns you into a sitting duck.

Let's make that hypothetical story a little more visible. Suppose the devil in that story was Lebron James, who had the same build, speed, and strength but wasn't in the NBA. He's that devil in the hood who chose a life of crime and violence. Now, put Lebron in that first scenario. If your only option to get away was to run, do you think you could outrun him with your pants sagging?

When I ask young men this, they say, "Yeah! I would dip on him, especially if my life were on the line!"

But let's be realistic. Imagine Lebron James with a full range of motion versus you running while pulling up your pants. I think, no, I know Lebron got you. I am as fast as they come, but I know it would be a wrap if I was sagging and had to get away from Lebron. I'm finished.

Flip the story and say you had to run from the cops. I'm not condoning running from the cops, nor should you have a reason to run from them, but what if you did? This story isn't that farfetched because there are so many victims of police brutality.

Why sag your pants and put yourself at a disadvantage? Young Black men, you are already a suspect in the eyes of the law. It's a sad but harsh reality that we face. Sagging your pants raises that suspicion to another level. For instance, if you had to run from an officer and hop a fence, the probability of you escaping is dramatically reduced due to you having to hold your pants up.

I get it, though. Maybe sagging is your way of rebelling against society. I understand that, but there are better ways to do it.

You can rebel against the system by showing your intellect, being healthy, and not having to depend on the health care system. You can learn how to spend money on meaningful products that benefit you and those around you.

Why rebel by following a fad that isn't even fashionable? Following this fad could get you thrown in jail, supporting the system you thought you were rebelling against. Which rebellion yields better results: sagging or using your intellect?

Plus, who are you showing your draws to? What would your grandma or grandpa think if they saw you sagging? Your grandma's thoughts of you should be of the utmost importance. You should never want to embarrass your grandma or those who came before you.

People say that sagging originated in jail. Inmates didn't intentionally sag their pants but had no choice because they weren't allowed to have belts for various reasons. Belts could be used as weapons or to commit suicide. This theory holds weight because the prison environment is a breeding ground for either scenario.

The other theory is that gay men in jail would sag to show that they were available. Both theories sound plausible, but no one knows where sagging originated. What I do know is that it needs to cease to exist.

Whether you are duck-walking down the street or in the mall, wherever you are, you look foolish. Wise men do wise things.

Plus, if we were to survey women who had their priorities in order, I am pretty sure the majority, if not all, would say that sagging is unattractive. So, if you want a grown and classy woman, I suggest you pull up your pants and show her that you have all your *ducks* in a row!

The Set Up

I took my sister and her friend out to eat not too long ago. After we ate, we talked a little bit and went home. As we approached the car, I noticed that the tires needed air. I told the queens we would fill them up before they hit the road. Who would have thought putting air in a car's tires would endanger our lives?

Before they left that night, we drove over to the gas station around the corner of my house. When we pulled up to the gas station, four young teenage males stood outside the door.

The gas station was directly in front of us, and the air pump was on the right side, located on a wall connected to the building. The wall was twenty yards long and reached the sidewalk, so you couldn't see anything or anyone as they approached. As I was getting out to pump the air, as usual for D.C., the young Black males asked me for some change.

I told them, "Naw! I only got what I need for this air."

I put my quarters in and began to pump the tires on the left side of the car, the side opposite the pump. As I was kneeling, two teenagers began to slap box and wrestle. I watched them from the corner of my eye but didn't think much because that's what young men do. It suddenly got strange when one of the young males walked to the air pump and stood there.

That's when my hood senses and intuition went off. At the same time, my sister's and Jessica's senses were going off, too. I didn't hear their conversation, but Jess asked my sister if she felt we were being set up.

She noticed one of the young males had gone and looked into the parked police car to see if a cop was in it. When he noticed that there wasn't a cop in the car, he waved for some people to come over from behind the wall. I didn't see the wave, but I did notice the barrage of people coming from nowhere.

Before we pulled into the gas station, I saw the cops walk into a pizza shop across the street. As I went to put air on the other side near the pump, my sister and Jess got out of the car. Victoria came around to the side where I was, and I told her she didn't have to get out.

"F*** that!" she told me, "You know I'm crazy as hell! I don't play that s***, and you know that I stay with mine!"

I laughed because I knew what she was out there to do. I continued to pump the air in the tire but never knelt entirely because I wanted to keep my eye on the dude standing by the pump and be ready for whatever may happen.

Time ran out, and I went to take the hose back to the pump; Victoria told me to throw it on the ground. She was watching the young boy sneakily watching me the whole time. Thankfully, we put the caps back on the tires and left without anything happening!

How did that story make you feel? Crazy, right?

What were their plans, and why did we all feel like we were being set up? How do we get young Black men to regain their critical thinking abilities? Why does it take someone to get hurt to see their error?

That day could have been some of those young men's very last. Victoria has no problem using her blade, especially if she and hers are in danger. I'm the same way in protecting mine, which is one of the reasons I stay physically fit. She is also the mother of my two nephews, whom I love dearly. I will do anything and everything to make sure that they're straight in life, including putting their mother's life over mine!

Jessica stays with the banger and is trained by the military to use it properly. But she didn't have it on her due to the uncertainty of not knowing where her license permits her to carry. That ended up being a good thing. I would've hated for her to have used it and left that on her conscience despite it being self-defense.

The three of us are all trained, skilled, ready, and able to protect and defend ourselves. These were fourteen-year-old scrawny males; my sister alone would have beaten a couple of them to death.

Let's say that we did have to take a kid's life that day. His mother would have been on the news crying and confessing to the world, "*My son was wonderful! He didn't deserve to die! He was an angel! He would never do anything to anyone!*"

Meanwhile, she knows that her son is a devil. He was a devil out there hitting licks and trying to set people up for a quick dollar. Many parents know that their kids live recklessly in the streets, but when the streets catch them, they want to act like everything is okay.

A lot of our young men never realize that they are setting up their lives to be full of hardships and failure, lives lived in and out of prison. They never think they may hit the wrong lick and lose their life.

The circle of life is one hundred percent true. What goes around comes right back around. Don't do it to someone else if you wouldn't want it done to you. It's that simple.

That street credit you think you are earning doesn't amount to respect. Genuine respect is earned, not given. You won't receive genuine respect standing at corner stores and gas stations all day.

It's time to redirect our kids' energy and stop letting these young men go astray.

To the young men reading this, know that anyone over twenty-one still chilling at corner stores likely doesn't have much going on in their lives. And they are leading you down the same path of nothingness and destruction. That isn't a person that you want to be around.

We have to come together and brainstorm ways to get these boys off the streets. If we took half the money we spent on clothes and other pointless materials and collectively put it together to build schools and recreational centers, we would be setting up a brighter future for all of us.

If you can offer a young Black male a job, please do so. Pay him whatever you deem necessary to clean up the litter around the block. By cleaning up his block, he will set a positive example for his peers and be less likely to litter himself now that he is the one who cleans it up.

This leads to the next chapter about hardened hearts.

Hardened Hearts

Are we living in an age where people's hearts, minds, and souls are so hardened that they do not want to see and hear the truth? I ask this because it's easy to tell where a person's heart is as soon as they open their mouth. When observing their actions, it is also easy to tell where a person's heart and mind are.

I ride the Metro to and from work every day. En route to work one day, I thoroughly inspected my seat as usual to ensure there wasn't anything on it. I noticed some trash on the floor, but nothing too unusual. So, I sat down.

Within two minutes of sitting down, a guy one seat up and across from me pulled out a leftover food box and placed it on the seat in front of me as if it were a trash can. I jumped to say something, but something told me to fall back, laugh, and shake my head.

As I laughed, I looked around at other people to see if anybody else felt what he did was inconsiderate. I was the only one laughing. I probably looked like the crazy one.

Many men have heavy and hardened hearts. That theory isn't that farfetched. That story exemplified where that man's heart and mind were. And it's not as if he's the only one.

A lot of Black people claim to be Christians who believe in God. They will tell you how God created the heavens and the earth and everything in them but will disrespect God, the same God they profess to love, by destroying the land with litter. The roads and sidewalks within many Black communities are lined with trash.

Instead of cleaning the streets ourselves, we wait for White people to clean them for us. Not realizing that once we see them cleaning the neighborhood, they plan to move in, and soon, you'll be moving out. It's called gentrification.

A man with a heart filled with love of self would not dishonor himself or his neighborhood by littering. He takes pride and joy in building what he has, even if it is a little.

But since the love of self has dissipated and the people's hearts have hardened, they elect not to take care of the land where they live.

If you don't love yourself, you surely won't love your neighbor, nor would you have a problem in taking thy neighbor's life. A neighbor doesn't necessarily mean someone living close to you. It means seeing yourself in someone else. Only a hardened heart could kill another man, especially one who looks like you.

It may seem like littering is no big deal, but it is. It shows a lack of consideration for other people. In the story earlier, someone else got on the Metro and had to move that box to sit down. What if the next person to sit there accidentally sat in some of the food's juices? What if they were on their way to an interview? Their whole day would've been messed up.

Some may say that the people don't feel as if the land is theirs, so why should they care if they litter anyway, being that we used to be enslaved people on this land? That's an understandable point to be made. But with a bit of soul-searching and research, you'll find out that the story of slavery didn't happen how it has been told to us over the years.

The way his-story has been taught to us is purposely taught to harden our hearts and minds. To put you in a mind-state of feeling defeated.

Feeling defeated shouldn't be the case. Your ability to read this shows our resilience and perseverance as a people. I gave a hint that the Moors and other people were already on this land before Cristobal Colon "discovered" it in "Slave Ship Mentality." There is way more than meets the eye. A little studying will open up a whole new world.

Don't spend all of your time trying to get money so that you can move out of the hood. If you do so, you'll never realize that the hood is a hidden gem. We have to take care of it. Play your part and keep your yard clean. Remember that Somebody's Watching, so please play your role in our awakening!

To the people who think I'm reaching by using the term "destroy" when speaking about littering, calm down, Sheila/Billy! I know significant things are happening that are destroying the earth and its atmosphere. But we have to fix our own homes (self) before we can fix anyone else's.

Be GREATful

I know times get tough and life gets rough, but be grateful. If you can read this, be grateful for your vision. If you can turn the page, be grateful for your ability to touch. If you have on headphones rocking out to your favorite music, be grateful for your ability to hear.

I've noticed that we have become so ungrateful. Most Americans have a roof over their heads and at least some bread in their stomachs.

We all know there are plenty of people around the world who don't even have a home or food to eat daily. We say we know these things, but we never act upon the information we have.

Americans have become the most wasteful society. We waste anything and everything that we get our hands on, especially food. My goal isn't just to bring awareness to world hunger but to bring hunger to your soul to want to be grateful for everything you have and don't have.

This epiphany of how ungrateful we are as people was revealed to me one day while riding the Metro home from work. Honestly, I don't like to wear headphones in public. To me, headphones take away the natural harmony of life. When I put them on, I try to ignore everything and everyone. (Be honest, we often wear our headphones to drown out other people.) This day, I put them on to do just that: drown out everybody because I had a hard day at work.

The Most High instantly knocked me down from my high horse when I noticed the man behind me boarding the train was in a mobile wheelchair. He was in business attire and had a briefcase on the side of his chair. It looked like he was traveling home from a long workday, just like the rest of us.

The only difference was that I was standing and able to walk. He was paralyzed from the neck down. He controlled his wheelchair with a white stick he wielded with his mouth. He used the very same stick to type on his phone.

It put a tear in my eye when I realized how self-absorbed I was by putting headphones on to ignore other humans.

The guilt and ungratefulness filled my heart when I realized how much I was complaining to myself. In my head, I was having conversations with myself like, *"Really, Cliff? Was your day that hard? Did you jump out of bed and dress yourself this morning? Are you not standing tall with full health and mobility? Oh! You are, huh! Well, be quiet then!*

But you might ask, "Cliff, what does that have to do with wearing headphones?"

I'll answer your question with a question. Do you put your headphones in your ears? More than likely, you do. The man in the wheelchair, who is not able to move his hands and feet, wakes up every day and goes to work. He doesn't walk to the Metro wearing his headphones every day. I don't know how he gets to the Metro, but I do know that his times are probably tough, and his life may be rough, but he still pushes through it daily.

Headphones have been a major component in dehumanizing humanity. We are no longer grateful for the ability to speak and communicate with one another. In a sense, we have become ungrateful for our own and other people's lives.

We complain about things in our lives that are within our power to change. Many of us walk around with an *I deserve better because it's me* attitude. We need to learn to appreciate the simple day-to-day things that we are capable of doing.

Maybe your clothes aren't the flyest, and your shoes aren't the freshest, but at least you have some. That is a good enough reason to be grateful. To be able to accept the things that you don't have shows a great deal of humility.

One thing I do, no matter who is around, is pick up pennies. Never be above anything or anyone because the moment you feel high and mighty on your horse, the real High and Mighty will knock you right back down.

When you are out in public, take time to people-watch. It is a wonderful thing to be able to see and appreciate the beauty of people. Appreciate life by being grateful that we even exist. Be GREATful!

How to Become More Goal-Oriented

Write down your goals. Writing down your goals is the first step toward accomplishing them. It takes your thoughts and turns them into action.

The next thing to do is buy a dry-erase board and write your goals on it. Place the dry-erase board on your refrigerator. You're placing it on the fridge because you eat every day. Therefore, you have no choice but to look at your goals and be reminded of them every time you go to the fridge.

Read your goals when you wake up every morning to help guide the direction of your day.

Please take a picture of your goals and make it your phone's screensaver. Also, make that picture your computer's screensaver. You will be forced to see your goals every time you use your phone and computer.

Seeing your goals and perpetually reading them makes them ingrained in your thought process. The more you think about something, the more you work to make that thought a reality.

Every single invention we see and use today started as a thought. Let's use a chair, for example. The person who invented the chair thought about it so much that they took the necessary steps to make the intangible thought into a tangible chair.

Your thoughts become your reality. Therefore, you should guard your mind against anything that deters you from reaching your goals. This isn't a selfish act. You cannot help others until you have helped yourself. We can only change ourselves for the better and hope our light shines on someone else, who will then change their life by following our example, hence the ripple effect.

I pray that you will be strong and that you will be successful in all of your future endeavors.

Slave Ship Mentality (S**t on N****s)

A presence was already here in America and all across the globe before Christopher Columbus "discovered" this land. But for this story's sake, I will use the history we've been told, so ride with me on this one.

As the story goes, Black peoples' ancestors were forced into ships. They were held captive with chains around their necks, wrists, and ankles. They were forced to lie on top and beside each other without any space to move.

To make matters worse, they were naked. The trip across the Atlantic Ocean from Africa to America, known as the Middle Passage, was not short. It may have taken anywhere from three to six months.

During this time, as all humans do, our ancestors had to defecate (s**t) and urinate. But they did not have the luxury of a toilet. When they went, it was on themselves or the person lying beside or beneath them. There were no other options. No matter how hard they tried to hold it in, it would have to come out sooner or later.

During slavery, our true heritage was systematically erased from our minds. But have we forgotten the recent history of slavery they hesitantly give us?

Let's fast forward to today. Today, all we hear in rap music is how this person got money, and now he

"S**t on n****s!" This person got cars, and now he "S**t on n****s!" He's wearing the latest fashion, so now he "S**t on n****s!"

Almost everything we do these days is a direct slap in the face of our ancestors and their trials and tribulations. So, before you buy clothes with a slave master's name on them, thinking you're about to S**t on n****s!

Remember this old saying. We're *all in the same boat!*

Men of Good Character

There will always be a friendly competition between men. We compete in everything we do, from working out to sports to business, playing Scrabble, or anything that can be calculated and summed up. That's just what we do. A little friendly competition is healthy. It forces those involved to try and be their best within the competition.

My brother Brad and I competed on the court not too long ago. You know how it goes. The older brother always has to beat on and show the younger brother he will never be able to stick with him. Since I'm a couple weeks older than Brad, I had to get my M.J. on and show him how I got these rings.

After a couple of games of me, Jesus Christing (I mean crossing) him, and his ankles were all sore and bruised. I'm joking. Brad and I played some good games. We went to the park to get another workout in. As Brad and I were doing pull-ups, a young male around five or six ran up to us and asked if he could do some pull-ups with us. We gladly obliged.

His mom walked behind him to keep her eyes on him, as all parents should. Brad and I were cordial and said hello to her. We only received a stank-faced response when we asked her how she was doing. We each were like, *okay*, then continued to coach and encourage the little man to keep pushing and pulling.

Before he could do a couple of pull-ups, his mom said, "Ahh, come on! Let's go!"

Of course, he said, "I want to stay and do some pull-ups!" But she was so mad at the world that she dragged him off, and they walked to her car.

It never crossed her mind that she may have been snatching away a spark of positivity from her son's life. He was excited to work out and even more excited to receive positive energy from older Black males. Younger males seek and yearn for attention from older males.

Gangs are a testimony of proof to the last paragraph. Most men in gangs are in them because they seek attention and love from a male figure, the attention that they may have never received at home.

Consequently, they find love in the streets. It's not real love, but you can't tell the difference when you have never felt the agape love of a father or father figure. Agape love is the highest form of love; it's sacrificial. Agape love will have a man take a bullet for his son. Street love will have you put a bullet in another man. Which love is real: agape or street?

A friend of mine, who I love and would do anything for, has a son. I've known her for a little over two years. She knows the content of my character and everything I am about. But it took me nearly two years to meet her young prince.

I understood why she doesn't want certain men around her son. When I think about how foul some guys have treated our women, I know why these same women may become suspicious toward all of us.

Women should discern the heart and character of every man they interact with. I, and men like me, are the type of men that should always be around young males. We are positive role models and the men who will ensure young men don't get out of line. We will be the ones that put one in his chest when he acts up. And I don't mean the street love way of a bullet, but rather, the agape love way of a fist.

Young men want to know that other men care about them enough to discipline them and teach them when they are in the wrong. After a while, a young male will lose that fear he once had of his mother. A woman whooping and hollering at her son just isn't enough. This is where a man of good character plays his role.

We live in an age where the *independent* woman mindset has swept the nation. There is nothing wrong with a woman being able to hold her own, work, and take care of business. I encourage that. I don't encourage an attitude of I can do everything without a man, especially to the detriment of our young males.

Please do not take this wrong. Plenty of single women raise amazing kids by themselves, and I applaud every one of you. But in an ideal world, women need men just as much as men need women. We balance each other out and make each other whole.

Plus, let's be honest, women, you don't have what little Anthony has downstairs. So, how will you show him how to use his pants' zipper properly? And I don't have what little Shenika has downstairs. So, how could I tell her how to use a pad properly?

That's the balance that kids need. Men and women of good character will also raise children of good character.

Love Cures All

"He who spares the rod hates his son, but he who loves him is careful to discipline him" (Proverbs 13:24). We must go back to the days when our communities were actual communities.

The elders talk about how, back in their day, if they got caught doing something wrong, the whole community, including teachers, neighbors, and elders, would discipline them. The elders also mention that when they got home, they would get it again from their parents.

These days, the elders seem scared or want nothing to do with today's youth.

A while back, I was in Baltimore riding on a bus that happened to be packed with high school students. They were loud and obnoxious as usual, but honestly, I don't have a problem with that. That's just what teenagers do. My only problem is that in this era, they don't have the same respect for elders as I did when I was their age.

When I was young, my boys and I acted up and were loud, but we knew when and where to modify our behavior. If we were in a public atmosphere, we tried our hardest not to cuss, and when we did cuss, we looked around for any elders to apologize to. I have noticed that many teens today don't do that anymore. They'll just let the filth fly out their mouths, disregarding who is around.

Foul language and fly words were happening at the back of this packed bus. I stood next to a guy who kept saying, "Stupid kids!"

I thought, "*They are acting stupid, but nothing will change if no one ever says anything to them.*" I wanted to make my way to the back, but the bus was overpacked to the point where the driver wasn't letting anyone else on.

All the students got off the bus at the next stop, and I missed an opportunity to say something. I don't know if it is just me and my love for youth, but I don't mind speaking and working with them. I love it.

Over the years, I realized that kids love being around me. They usually listen to what I have to say. Maybe it's because I look young and still dress youthfully, but kids want to know that the people around them really care for them. Even when I give a kid tough love, they know it is love.

Love is how we bridge the disconnect between our youth and elders. We have to bring back a sincere love for one another.

To the elders, you have to realize that most of the time, young people aren't going to walk up to you and ask for advice. You have to be the bold one. A few kids may brush you off, but there will always be those looking for guidance.

We should aim to say something encouraging to a young person every day. Call a random young lady a "princess." I bet it brightens up her day. A lot of kids today have never been complimented. I am living proof that this method works.

I had previously said, "Excuse me, young queen!" to this teenage girl because I needed space to get by her, and she lit up.

Walking by, I heard her say to her friends, "Aww!!! No one has *ever* called me that before!" I will make it a requirement that I call a young woman a "queen" and a young man a "king" every day.

If we continue to shower children with positive and uplifting messages, it will eventually change how they view the world and how the world views them. We must make sure that we do it with love. Real love will cure us.

Go Hard Or Die Easy

G.H.O.D.E

Matthew 7:13-14 in the Bible says the following:

Enter through the narrow gate. For wide is the gate, and broad is the road that leads to destruction, and many enter through it.
But small is the gate, and narrow is the road that leads to life, and only a few find it.

The motto *Go Hard or Die Easy* means going hard in everything you do to improve yourself **mentally**, **spiritually**, and **physically**. The mental, spiritual, and physical all coexist and play as a team. You are only as strong as your team's weakest link.

A friend of mine kept telling me to have *tunnel vision*. He explained that having tunnel vision means staying focused on your goals and never losing sight of them.

Matthew 7:14 tells us that the path to life is "difficult." Some might say that it is difficult to eat healthily, but if you don't take the difficult route and eat healthy food, your body will sooner or later die easily from illnesses and diseases.

Some people might also say that studying is difficult, but if you don't study, your mind will weaken and die easily. A weak mind can't focus on the spiritual things it needs to do to improve; therefore, the spirit dies easily.

The Bible also says:

Many will say to me on that day. 'Lord, Lord, have we not prophesied in Your name and done many wonders in Your name?"
And then I will declare to them, "I never knew you, depart from Me, you who practice Lawlessness!"
(Matthew 7: 22-23)

A lot of people would rather live in bliss and continue in their ignorance, which is defined as lacking knowledge. They never realize that living in bliss is the easy path that leads to destruction; therefore, they never *ask, seek, and knock* on the door that leads to life.

These verses aren't me pounding a Christian religion in your head. You must learn from everything you read to better your life, whether it is the Bible, Quran, Metu Neter, The Kybalion, or The Emerald Tablets.

I like to use the Bible because it is an easy reference point for most people. But then again, as these verses tell us, many people only want to call on The Most High when they are going through the fire.

You must study to show yourself approved. To be approved, you should abide by the motto of Go Hard or Die Easy! These are the only two options we have in life. Which option will you choose?

Don't Let Father Time Catch You Slipping

I'd like to give a shout-out to Father Time
He waits on no man
I'd also like to give a shout-out to Mother Nature
Because she's where these people are going to be
Sooner than they know it
For waiting on Father Time

Never put it off until tomorrow; what you can do today. Many of us procrastinate and say things like, "I work better under pressure." Pressure, at times, will bring out the best in us. But a lot of times, we put ourselves in unnecessary stressful situations.

We wait until the day before a **dead**line to try and accomplish the task at hand. If we were honest, we could and would accomplish so much more. Procrastination puts us in a world of trouble.

We procrastinate because of fear. I found this out while standing at the bus stop during college. This lady randomly started talking to me about what I was doing. I told her that I was in college and on my way to finish a paper before class.

She said, "So you waited until the last minute to work on the paper?"

I told her the excuse we all use, "Yeah, I do my best work at the last minute!"

I was serious. I thought I was like Superman, who could do anything when the pressure was on. Boy, that lady hit me with some wisdom I would never forget.

She told me that procrastination was a spirit of fear. We procrastinate to give ourselves a cop-out. Many of the papers I wrote in college could have been much better if I had put more time and energy into them. I procrastinated because of my fear of failure.

For example, let's say I turn in a paper I worked on at the last minute and receive a lousy grade. I now have an excuse as to why. I can tell myself that I didn't do too well because I worked on it at the last minute. But when I get the okay or good grade, I'll keep telling myself that *I'm good at working under pressure*. In actuality, I did a mediocre job.

The fear is of doing your best and not receiving the outcome you wanted. But that shouldn't be a fear that you hold onto. You will never know until you know. Then, when you do know, it still isn't a failure; it is a learning experience.

You get out what you put in. That is a universal law.

I pray that from this moment forward, you use Father Time wisely.

Just Masturbate

Just beat it. Go ahead and beat it as soon as you wake up in the morning, beat it before you eat breakfast, beat it before you eat lunch, beat it in the daytime, beat it before you eat dinner. And you know you have to beat it right before you sleep. If you answered yes, I would say that you were right, but not in the way you may be thinking.

Let me give you a little mental clarity. Many things in this life are a façade. Words have been twisted in this system to have us thinking one way when we should be thinking another. For instance, this chapter's title and opening paragraph probably made you think I was telling you to pleasure yourself throughout the day, but I am telling you to do the opposite.

When you learn their etymology, words have several different meanings. Etymology studies the origin of words and how their meanings have changed throughout history.

Masturbate can be divided into two words: mastur (master) and bate (bait). To *master* something is to overcome or conquer it. *Bait* is a trap or temptation.

Temptation dangles in front of our faces every day. When we turn on the TV, we see the bait. When we turn on the computer, we see the bait. When we open a magazine, we see the bait. All this bait is dangled in front of us to keep our minds and energy only focused on sex. This system keeps our minds and energy stuck on our lower selves.

The system will tell you to masturbate by its definition of the term, which is to stimulate one's genitals for sexual pleasure. That's why they call it Mastur**bait**: you usually end up *hooked* once you do it. We've all succumbed to that bait like a fish out of water. The goal is to see that bait and go the other way.

There are right and wrong ways to have sex. Masturbation, by this world's standards, is the wrong way. Every time you "choke your chicken," you lose a piece of your essence. Your energy is drained. Your power and clarity of mind dissipate.

The other bait they throw in our faces daily is the temptation to eat bad food. If you watch TV, you are constantly bombarded with junk food commercials. While driving down the street, you see billboards directing you to these places.

Fast food places lead to the destruction of our bodies. When I said, "Beat it before breakfast; beat it before lunch; beat it before dinner," I was referring to the junk food temptation. The lure to eat junk food is one of the strongest daily temptations. Mastering this bait will make your body feel amazing.

Suppose you have goals you would like to accomplish or a dream you would like to live; try to master bait (beat temptation) the correct way just for one week as an experiment. I'm willing to bet that if you stay strong and resist the temptation, your mind's eye will become clearer. Your foresight and natural intuition will become stronger as well. Obstacles and problems will become much easier to solve. Your creativity will start to rise and go back to the days when you were a child.

To Master Bait (beat temptation), you must know yourself, your strengths, and your weaknesses. Once you have learned your weaknesses, you can work on them and turn them into strengths.

After the first week, extend it to three weeks of mastering bait. I promise you will become much stronger. You will be an unstoppable person who can accomplish anything you put your mind to.

EXPRESS Yourself

Self-expression is a must. But when our vision of self has been so diluted that our expression has become convoluted, it's time to reevaluate where we are and where we are headed.

The other day, I walked down Alabama Ave. and passed a young man around nineteen. I looked at him in the face and eyes to show recognition; as usual, it wasn't reciprocated. As I got closer, I noticed he was doing some crazy sag, where his shirt was tucked in or extremely tight.

He was showing the front of his underwear. He had on EXPRESS underwear. This was his intention, though. He wanted people to know the brand of his underwear, hence his crazy sag. I was confused. He looked like he was trying to EXPRESS himself as a gangster, but his expression didn't make sense.

A lot of young men walk around trying to be the biggest gangsters and tough guys but will have a gay designer's name and logo wrapped around their waist. That's what we call an *oxymoron*. More importantly, when you sag, you look like a *moron* when you need to look like a Moor.

Let me ask you this: Does life imitate art, or does art imitate life? Fashion is a form of art. Since we are so culturally deprived of our heritage and knowledge of self, we do and wear everything that has been given to us by the same people that wiped away our culture.

From the language we speak, the clothes we wear, and the messiah we praise, our lives imitate White people's art. You cannot honestly tell yourself or me that when you *first* think of Jesus, you do not see a White man. The image of Cesare Borgia is ingrained in our psyches because someone knew that life imitates art.

The confusion within our community can be healed. Knowledge and wisdom will pull us from our current state of sleep. Knowledge of self will make anyone want to wear clothes and do things beneficial for themselves and the people they represent.

We have to go back to expressing ourselves in our true nature. We have to quit being scared of being labeled or tagged as being "too Black." There is nothing wrong with self-expression. Expression of self does not mean we hate others; it simply means we appreciate and respect ourselves and those who came before us. When we express this art form, true healing will come.

By reading this book, you can tell that I express myself through writing, working out, drawing, and speaking to people. How do you **express** yourself?

Do We Really Want Change?

As I write this, it seems we don't want change. We like to scream, fuss, and holler in the streets about change, but we don't really want it. Babies and children scream, fuss, and holler. It's called a temper tantrum. These marches and riots are adult temper tantrums. We have so much more work to do to change our situation.

Let's work on building from the ground up. No one is stopping us from growing food, producing clothes, learning how to conduct electricity, building houses, or anything else.

There will always be opposition. All the Black Wall Streets across the country showed us that, but challenges shouldn't be used as excuses for why we can't rebuild and try again. We should look at them as learning experiences.

Not to take anything from the greatness of our ancestors, but they marched fifty to sixty years ago, and where did it get them or us? Integration? During segregation, we had more love for one another. Because we knew that we had to stick together to survive. We wanted to build and support our businesses and families. After integration, we lost our love for ourselves and all of the dignity and respect that came with it.

By continuing to march, it's as though we expect people who have never loved us to all of a sudden love us because we are walking in the streets while waving signs in the air. It's ludicrous and a slap to our ancestors' faces not to have learned from our past.

There is no reason for a cop to murder any young Black man or woman, nor am I justifying it, but why aren't we marching every single day in the streets of Wilkinsburg when a young Black man takes another young Black man's life? I'll ask again: how do you expect someone who has never loved you to love you, and you don't even love yourself?

If we had genuine love and respect for ourselves, we would not need to march and riot in the streets. Imagine if all Black men stood together. Do you think any cop would disrespect one of us without fearing the consequences of his actions? These murders that we see at the hands of these officers would cease to exist if we stood in solidarity.

Have you ever noticed that deaths by cops of other nationalities don't seem to happen or aren't reported as often? Let one too many Mexicans die at the hands of police officers; I'm scared to even think about what a cartel may do. Same thing with Asians and their mafias. People of other races and ethnicities stick together and go to war for each other as a family should.

Can you see how knowledge and a love of self are the only things that will change our situation? We wouldn't even be in this predicament if we had true knowledge and love for ourselves. We would walk differently. We would talk to and treat each other differently. We would rarely have to interact with the police because they would not be needed. We would police our blocks.

The only way to gain such knowledge is to turn off the television and music and study. Read more books, work out, and eat better. Take care of your body.

Rioting and marching in the streets will only lead to more deaths of our people. The police have already shown us they are willing to pull the trigger. The curfews they have enforced showed that martial law is real. Now, if the police aren't scared to pull the trigger on you, do you think the military will be?

The powers that be know if we were to wake up and realize the greatness and beauty within, we would change this whole system overnight. That is why they are **purposely** broadcasting and having all these attacks. They want to get us to act out on emotion and not logic. Emotions lead to riots; logic and intellect lead to a power struggle.

The Sidewalk Law

What happened to the days when a man would walk down the street, approach another man, look him in the eye, and say, "Hello," or give a head nod? People used to walk by each other, tip their hats, and say, "Good Day!" as recognition that another person had crossed their path.

Is it me, or does it seem like all the codes, ethics, laws, and morals we used to live by have gone with the wind? Nowadays, it is almost as if we go out of our way not to engage other people. We try our hardest not to look at people passing by as we walk down the sidewalk.

I have noticed a couple of things that people do. The first thing they do is play on their phones. Or they will try to use all their mental energy to keep their heads and eyes straight. I am confused when people look me in the eye, and I nod or say, "How are you?" but get no response. It's like, really, though, you didn't hear or see me.

We're all on "social" media, but we don't have any social skills.

Here are a few sidewalk laws that we must relearn. For the men out there, the first law is that when *walking with your lady friend, make sure that she is on the inside.* You should always be the one closest to the street. This is to prevent anything that may happen, like a car jumping the curb. You can push her out of the way and hopefully dodge the accident yourself. It also prevents rainwater from splashing up and ruining that nice outfit it took your lady an hour or two to put together.

Another reason to have your lady on the inside is to signal to all the onlookers that she is walking with a man. People driving by will likely see you, and their thirst for your beautiful lady will die down. It won't disappear, but it will lessen. There will always be dehydrated people out here.

The second law is *that traffic flow follows the same flow as cars*. Stay to the right.

The third law is to *share the sidewalk*. It's amazing how many times I've encountered people walking in groups who don't know how to line up with each other to let the person approaching have space to walk by.

The fourth law, and maybe the most important, is to *always look people in the eyes and show recognition as you walk by them*. A simple nod would suffice, but if you choose to speak, that's even better. The reason why this one is so important is that the eyes are the gateway to the soul. For example, if you and I are strangers, and one day we cross each other's path, if we look at each other and give a simple head nod, now we recognize each other's face.

If I happen to cross your path in the future and you need help, I would be more inclined to help you, just from the one time we made eye contact. In my head, I'd think, "*Oh, that's that one guy/girl that lives around the way from me that I saw however long ago. Let me go see if they need my help.*"

To the ladies, I guess you do have to be a little more cautious about the last law. Use your discernment. They say not to judge a book by its cover, but we judge books by their covers daily. Look at a man in his eyes, and you will see his intentions. Just know that every guy who says hello isn't trying to be on or approach you. There are still some cordial fellows out here who are just following the fourth law.

Are You Planning for Your Kids' Future?

How are you raising your kids? As a Black father who can't get a job because the system is set up to make it difficult for you to obtain one, are you raising your kids to be leaders and employers (not employees)?

Are you cultivating their minds with math, science, business acumen, history, and knowledge of self? Or are you one of those parents who allow your kids to watch and learn about life through a TV, cell phone, or tablet screen? Do you buy your kids everything you never had growing up?

We have to start raising our children to be better than we are. I will repeat this later: You are your children's god. Too many people give their kids options, not realizing that what they say is the *only* option a kid has. If you pay attention to history, you will notice that most people who are great at something had parents who taught them certain values at a young age.

For example, Venus and Serena Williams are some of, if not the greatest tennis players to walk this earth. One thing they had, along with other great people, was a strict parent. Their father instilled the value of hard work, dedication, and determination at a young age. Teaching his kids those values was an investment in their and their family's future.

I used the Williams sisters as an example because they are great at tennis, disciplined, and intelligent enough to run businesses.

Let's cultivate our children's minds to be great at everything they put their time and dedication to.

Listen to Your Body

I love to work out, exercise, stretch, and do anything that will make me feel and look healthy. I love the energy it gives me. I love that feeling after a workout. You know that feeling you get when your muscles are tight, and that tightness tells you that you just put in work? It's a beautiful feeling.

The after-workout feeling is so wonderful that I often feel as if I should work out again right after I have finished working out. There have been plenty of times when I was working out and felt a minor pain and continued to work through it, only to injure myself.

As I have grown in years and hopefully wisdom, I have learned to relax and not be so gung-ho all the time. An injury can put me on a hiatus from working out anywhere between a week to a month.

More than likely, you have been on a hiatus from working out in your lifetime due to an injury you could've prevented if you had only listened to your body. Not working out or exercising is more painful mentally than the actual injury.

These days, I listen to my body and assess the situation. If my body tells me to stop, I stop. By stopping, I am preventing further injuries and giving my body the time it needs to heal. By preventing future injuries, you will progress further and have less mental strife.

Some tweaks and twitches can be stretched out and fixed right there on the spot. Assess the situation by listening to your body. You should listen to your body before you listen to music. Some may say they need music to work out, but what did people do before headphones and technology?

Silence will help you learn and know your body's rhythm and pace. Exercising without music is a great way to clear your mind and work through your thoughts.

After This Book, Grab Another One

All the answers to our problems are right in front of our faces! But somehow, we haven't been able to solve them. We haven't been able to pull ourselves out of oppression because we have not read and studied enough to take our minds to a level of complete freedom.

A lot of people are only able to read just enough to be able to order something off the McDonald's menu. That sounds harsh, but it's real. This is not written to offend anyone. We have to address real problems that are plaguing our communities. If you know someone who can't read, teach them quietly.

We've all heard the age-old saying, "If you want to hide it from a n***a, put it in a book!" Did that saying come from nowhere? Is it just a stereotype, or is it true? A brother of mine recently told me about the 50/500 rule. The rule states that Black men will spend $500 per year on the outside of their heads (i.e., haircuts and hats) instead of fifty dollars per year on the inside (i.e., buying books and documentaries).

What he said hit me hard because I thought about our warriors, writers, visionaries, scholars, activists, and ancestors who have written books on our plight. However, we still haven't risen from our situation.

It's going to take time to psychologically heal from all of the wicked things that have been done to us throughout history. I am sure we would heal ourselves if we cracked open and read more books!

Books contain answers from people who have gone through and overcome problems you are going through now. That is the meaning of the phrase, "There is nothing new under the sun!" You won't be the first or the last to go through what you're going through.

Turn off and ***unplug*** your TV. It is clinically insane for anyone to subject themselves to such negative images of themselves. You will always be oppressed if you continue to let someone else dictate the things that enter your mind.

Be an Everyday Hero

I walked through a parking lot not long ago and noticed a mother and her son walking toward their car. The mom turned left behind her truck, but her little man kept walking. He walked to the right and moved farther and farther into the middle of the aisle.

I was already a little cautious while watching him. My cautiousness paid off because a car started to back out of the parking spot.

I ran up screaming, "Hey! Hey! Hey! Hey! Hey! Hey! Hey!" trying to get the mom to grab her son and pull him out of harm's way.

The car never backed up close enough to hit the child, but it could have. The boy was one or two years old, and young boys are known for just running off. That is what boys do: explore.

When I got around the car, the young man's mother stood there smiling. She thanked me, and I told her it was no problem. We have to look out for our little ones.

I looked at the little man and said, "What's up?" Then, I looked back at his mother, told her to have a blessed day, and kept it moving.

Before I could even take two steps, a lady and her children walked by me, looked at me, and said, "That was good! That was good of you!"

I smiled at her and told her and her family to have a blessed day!

Would you have done the same thing? Are other people's kids your responsibility? A lot of people wouldn't want a stranger to say anything to their child, but when does the African proverb *It takes a village to raise a child* come into play?

While riding with my father one day, we passed a hoop court with some young men playing basketball. I slowed down to watch a little bit of the game. My dad quickly told me that I shouldn't have done that because some people may have viewed it wrongly. I understood where he was coming from, but I had no ill intentions or negative thoughts. And neither should other people.

When will we stop listening to negative news and trash television that is meant to keep us in constant negative and fearful thinking? When will we go back to admiring and putting honorable people at the forefront? We will never see the light in people if we always portray the darkness.

Let's build things that promote positive people and positive things. Let's work to change the false and negative perception of us that has been promoted so heavily in the media. Go out and be that hero!

Shine Brighter!

Strive hard to avoid things and people who are not about progress. Every day, do something to better yourself! Eat healthy (vegetarian/plant-based diet). Watch what happens after eating healthy. You will have more energy.

With more energy, you'll work out, exercise, and stretch more, giving you a better and healthier body! A healthy body has a healthy mind, and a healthy mind reads more books. Now your soul is shining!

Don't be one of those people who do dumb stuff every day and then get mad when they have to face the consequences of their actions. Please don't be angry at people reaping the rewards of their hard work. In this lifetime, you get what you put in. Some people might say that isn't true because they are hard workers. But who are you working hard for?

If you work hard for a job you do not love, you are working hard to build another person's enterprise or legacy. That doesn't mean you should start slacking off at work. It means that you should take some time out of your day, every day, to find and work on what you're passionate about.

The Most High has put us all here to shine.

Mystery – My Story – Mastery

A little while back, a few of my friends were upset that all of the images they see on TV and in movies are White characters. I understand where they are coming from, but I don't share in their anguish simply because I write and don't watch TV, so it doesn't bother me. I also understand that the people controlling everything you see and hear in the media write.

If I were to write a story or movie, it would feature primarily Black characters. That is My Story or the Mystery of Me. You can't be mad at someone for wisely using their time and brain to write his-story. You should be madder at yourself for not doing the same!

They say winners write history, which isn't necessarily true; it's just that the people who choose to write are writing his-story. No man or woman in their right mind would write their story and portray themselves as the loser.

So, I'll ask you to grab a pen and pad and start writing. Write whatever comes to mind. Write about how your day went. Write about all the thoughts and emotions that come to you. Write about the things you see and the troubles you went through. Write about everything.

Writing plays a significant role in conquering yourself. This is where self-mastery comes in. The world will be in your palm once you conquer yourself (Mastery).

To emphasize the importance of writing, I will drive the point home with this: The Quran and the Bible were **written**. Most of the world follows them or thinks they follow them.

Many of your favorite musicians write their music, and look at how big of a following they have. Please do not negate the importance of writing. I pray you start your writing journey now because writers rule the world!

How will your mystery be told? Don't let someone else write it for you.

There's a Lesson to be Learned Through Pain

We are here to experience and live life fully while learning new lessons. We should learn something new with every situation we go through.

The latest lesson I learned was taught through pain. It taught me a valuable lesson about myself and people in general. Pain in any form, whether physical or emotional, takes you away from being who you truly are. The latest pain that I went through was that of a physical injury.

Being injured not only didn't feel good, but it also put me on a hiatus from living life. I couldn't run and ride my bike every day. I went on a hiatus from working out for two weeks; therefore, I wasn't releasing endorphins, leaving me with built-up aggression and anger.

During those two weeks, my attitude wasn't the happy, goofy, loving Cliff everybody knows me to be. I had changed and become mean and rude to others.

My body had to heal for me to learn my lesson.

My mood and character instantly brightened as soon as I healed, and that's when I realized that people act out toward others because they are living in some form of pain, a pain they can't bear. They may be lashing out in anger that looks like it is directed at you, but it may be anger toward themselves.

Imagine feeling excruciating pain every time you wake up and get out of bed. You wouldn't be the happiest. A lot of us attempt to mask our pain, but it comes out in some form or another. When someone acts out of character and feels like they are coming at you wrong, remember not to take it personally. They may not be mad at you. They may be angry at themselves.

For people experiencing physical pain due to injury, my best advice is to use the R.I.C.E. method: rest, ice, compression, and elevation.

For those experiencing pain from an illness or disease, most illnesses end with itis (e.g., arthritis, conjunctivitis, colitis, etc.). This may mean that you are feeling some inflammation.

One of the best things you can do is detox, flush, and cleanse your system the herbal way or eat abundant vegetables, fruits, and nuts while drinking a lot of water. You may also be allergic to something you are eating. Remember, most food in today's grocery stores is made with profit in mind, not the consumer's health.

To those of you going through mental or emotional pain that seems too big of a burden, remember that no burden is placed on your shoulders that you can't handle. The answer and cure for mental and emotional pain are buried within yourself, as are all answers in life. Only you know the true reason why you feel the way you do, and only you know the answer to feeling better. You can always seek solace with your friends and family.

As I mentioned in "Mystery – My Story – Mastery," writing can be another great outlet to help work through mental and emotional pain. Writing is a great way to work through mental problems.

Writing this book and expressing what has worked for me and will prayerfully work for you has provided a self-analysis. It has been therapeutic.

Please write your story so that you may help yourself and others.

Destiny with Divinity

If I were to tell you the whole story of my life, you probably wouldn't believe some things. I've noticed that people admire people they think may have themselves together. A lot of people are so down on themselves that they would rather watch other people who seem to be up.

This is one of the reasons so many people are glued to the television. They crave that false sense of reality that television portrays, never realizing that as soon as the cameras are off, people on TV experience everyday trials and tribulations just as much as the next man or woman.

Hopefully, reading this book has helped you re-learn who you are. Please learn to prioritize what matters most to you, putting you in the driver's seat.

There should be no more sitting around watching other people live and enjoy their lives when you have a life to live. The people you watch on television take the time to accomplish their goals and get to where they are. Why sit around and watch them when you have your own goals to accomplish?

Let's work on not having so much despair and disbelief in ourselves and our God-given abilities. Everything is possible with just a little faith in yourself.

This story began by telling you that you wouldn't believe My Story if I told it to you. Like everyone else, I went through and still go through trials and tribulations daily, but I do not let those things keep me from fulfilling my destiny with divinity! And neither should you.

"You Go, Boy!"

Have you ever noticed how older women look at you and give you a smile of love when they see you are respectably carrying yourself? Maybe you don't know about the look that I'm talking about. Maybe you have never seen that grin of accomplishment and hope on an elder's face when they look at you with that "You Go, Boy!" smile.

A lot of us have failed to show our young men the way. To those who have been trying, keep on pushing. It will pay off. To the young men searching for a better way, I pray this book helps shine a light on a clear path. Every day should be a day to receive that "You Go, Boy" smile.

A few of my closest friends and I have concluded that many women love to see a young man who is focused. We all have shared the same story of how an elder has looked at us, smiled, and even sparked a conversation to see where our minds are.

Women love to see men dressed in uniforms, and they also love to see men dressed extremely dapperly. By extremely dapper, I mean dressed in clothes that fit well. (A belt is an accessory; it shouldn't be needed).

I told my brother, "Our women love to see us focused."

All I heard in the background from my sister was, "Amen!"

Our women want/crave to be able to say or even think, "You Go, Boy!" when they see us. Social media has shown us that our men and women are divided. Nowadays, our women rarely think, let alone say, "You Go, Boy!" to many of us. Our women aren't happy with what they see and hear from our men. A lot of them are upset and do not feel protected by us.

You rarely see young men with the creative hustle and drive these days. That same grind and hunger I had when I was younger isn't there anymore. Young Black males need to know that older women will throw money at them if they see that they are young, respectable, and focused.

My mother had a ten by fifteen square foot yard. It was starting to look horrendous. Of course, I cut it every time I went home, but I wouldn't have had to if these young men were on their grind. My momma would love to give young men money for doing something respectable. She would even throw in extra money just for the "You Go, Boy!" factor. That is just my mom. There are thousands upon thousands of other women just like her.

Young men, it's time to start thinking of new ways to hustle. Forget about all the false stories some rappers sell you about how they made it from selling drugs. That is an illusion that will only keep you trapped in a box.

Become a real hustler. If you open your eyes to see it as such, there is a lot of opportunity in the hood alone. Go back and read the chapter "Hardened Hearts." The community is waiting to be fixed and cleaned up.

Don't make excuses about not being able to afford a weed whacker or other equipment. If you or someone in your family can afford a pair of Jordans, they can afford to buy you whatever equipment you need to get your grind on.

Even if you had to buy an electrical weed whacker, I'm sure people wouldn't mind letting you use their electricity because they see you as someone with a vision of being and doing something great.

There are so many other ways to grind other than lawn care legally. I am just using that as an example of my experience when I was young. When I was thirteen, my friend Jason and I made a couple hundred dollars a day doing lawn care work.

We were doing it so much that WTAE Channel Four News interviewed us and aired our story on the evening news. All my friends and teachers asked us questions the next day at school. My mom's friends called her to tell me, "You Go, Boy!" You shine brighter when you are focused and doing something respectable.

My momma, sisters, aunts, and women always look at me with that "You Go, Boy!" smile because I am focused. My question to you is, are you?

Respect Her G!

After spending the day with my family, I decided to head back to the hotel to get some rest, but before my mom took me to the hotel, we stopped at a fast-food drive-thru. I'm not going to name the food chain because there aren't any free ads over here (lol), plus eating fast food isn't my thing; this was just a fly-by situation. Nonetheless, there are no excuses.

As I pulled up to the window, I noticed a beautiful young lady handing the food to the person taking the order so the person could hand it over to the car.

I'm guessing that my voice intrigued her. When this beauty heard me speaking to the clerk, she looked in the car as she handed over the first bags of food, and we locked eyes. I was intrigued as well. As she handed over the second bag of food, I noticed that the interest had completely died. As I pulled off, I wondered what could've happened and why she got cold so quickly.

I forgot that my nephews were in the back seat, and the second food bag contained two kids' meals. She could've thought the two kids' meals were for my kids. But when I realized that it was too late, I had pulled off. All I could do was laugh at the situation with my mom. There was no way for her to know they weren't my kids. But I respect her, G!

I respect her G because she was a woman with standards. She didn't want to deal with a man who had baggage unless it was packed and ready for them to go on a vacation. She was a woman working toward her goals and wouldn't let anyone or anything get in her way.

Please don't take what I am saying out of context. Kids are not baggage. Kids are beautiful, artistic, and creative souls. One of my ultimate goals is to bring life into this world with the right person.

A fair number of women deal with douchebags; unfortunately, they do so at their own will. Women must learn to read what others, especially men, say. The words from a man's mouth will ultimately show you where his heart lies.

Are his conversations only based on sex and other mundane things? Does he speak of the future and goals you two could accomplish if you became a union? Does he attempt to improve your life, or is he holding you back? Does he respect you?

The signs are there. Pay attention and do not ignore them, hoping to change that man. If he doesn't respect your G, fall back and be patient while waiting for the man who will.

Listen, Watch, and Speak Carefully!

You are what you watch and listen to. You bring into fruition the things that you speak about. These things are usually at the forefront of your mind and guide it somewhere. If television and music are that "somewhere" that your thoughts are focused on, those thoughts will soon become your reality. We must learn how to guard our hearts and minds.

Watching TV may seem harmless, but the harm it causes is endless. TV bombards your mind with subliminal and filthy messages. You may see a commercial for junk food and think nothing of it until, one day, you have a random craving for it.

Let's say you succumb to the temptation of eating junk. Once you've put that food into your body, you have just made room for diseases and all kinds of illnesses to invade and attack you and your health.

We must also learn to listen carefully to the people we converse with. I have had many people tell me that music does not influence them. After I explain the reasons as to why I know that it does, if they are not willing to listen, I end the conversation.

This is the part where you must listen carefully because if I continue to go back and forth with such a person, I would only be bringing myself to their level.

Proverbs 26:4 says, "Do not answer a fool according to his folly, or you will be like him yourself."

When people speak with you, they implant their ideals and beliefs. You must be wise enough to decipher the things being said to you, or you will succumb to the same lifestyle/problems as the person speaking.

Let's return to music and its control over us. For those who think it has no control, the next time you are around a teenager, ask them to solve a simple math equation and pay attention to how long it takes them to solve the question or if they even attempt to.

After that, ask them to spit the lyrics to the latest song. I'm willing to bet that they spit it back instantly. Music stays in your mind forever. That's why we were taught the alphabet through song.

It's easy to see the influence that music has on us. I am one hundred percent sure that I can ride the Metro any day and find a young bull walking up and down the car with his headphones on, singing his music out loud with his arms swinging, pants sagging, all while holding his genitals. I occasionally grab myself to readjust but not to look like I'm starring in a video.

People are what they listen to. The reality of a young man like that has become that of a rapper today. He, along with millions of others, listens to music and then sings it out loud; by singing it out loud, they are speaking it into their lives.

I'll use myself as an example. I was riding in my friend's car a while back, and he put on a Young Jeezy and Jay-Z track. I like to think I am a strong-willed individual, but after listening to that track, I even wanted to pick up a pie and get it booming. I say that no matter who you are, music influences you.

In the Bible, John 1:1 says, "In the beginning was the word . . ." Genesis 1:3 says, "and God said . . . " This could only mean that the Most High *spoke* things into existence.

I am not telling you to stop listening to music completely—I know that's hard to do—but just be very mindful about the music you ingest. Is it leading you on a path of destruction or building?

If we were made in the image of our Creator, we have the same ability to create as our Creator does. Therefore, we should **listen**, **watch**, and **speak** carefully in our daily lives.

This knowledge is not only written in the Bible. It is written on the walls (hieroglyphics) and in your DNA. You have to tap back into being who you truly are. Speak nothing less of being a god or a goddess about yourself.

Put Your Health First!

Most of us have been duped into putting more time, money, and energy into our secondary mode of transportation than our first. We will put more time and effort into making sure that our car is clean on the inside and out, but we won't do the same for our bodies, which are our main and first mode of transportation.

We get our car's oil changed, fluids flushed and refilled, washed and waxed, but we forget the last time we detoxed our bodily fluids. People have told me that they don't like the taste of water or that they don't ever feel like exercising or working out. Of course, you don't feel like being active because your body is filled with dirty oil, and it's time to change it.

Our temple is our prized possession. Our body is like our car; when you don't maintain it, it will break down sooner or later. We never purposely pour sugar into our car's tank. Then, we damn sure shouldn't pour it into our temple's tank. Dehydration and sugar cause most of the diseases we suffer from in today's world.

If we want to heal, we must drink more water. We should drink half our body's weight in ounces every day. For example, if you weigh 150 pounds, you should drink seventy-five ounces of water daily. If you want to go all out, shoot for a gallon of water.

We must walk more. People in other countries walk miles upon miles every day. Their society doesn't suffer from obesity and other diseases as much as Americans do. Plus, walking gives you time to think to yourself. Listen to the sound of nature while breathing the fresh air; in turn, you will be cleansing your lungs.

We will win in many other ways once we start putting our health first. We will have much joy, peace, happiness, love, prosperity, kindness, and overall well-being.

You Do Have Something to Prove

Live life like you have something to prove because you do. You have to prove something to yourself! Conquer yourself and become great at whatever it is you seek to become great at. The two hashtags below should help you to see clearly.

#TunnelVision

You must focus and envision your goals with a clear mind. To see clearly and think critically, cut out distractions (e.g., external forces such as music, television, and people).

#GoHardOrDieEasy

Everything worth attaining in life comes with hard work. Ask yourself if you really want it, and be honest. Many times, we say that we want to do and accomplish certain things, but we do not back up our words with actions.

What are your actions saying about you if actions speak louder than words? Be honest!

If You're Going to Play the Game, Play It to Win!

"When I was talking Instagram… The last thing you wanted was your picture snapped." – From Jay-Z's *Somewhere in America*.

I do not condone selling drugs, but think about it; if that's what you do, why do you have social media?

When combined, Facebook (FB) and Instagram (I) make the F.B.I. These days, there is no need for any law enforcement agency to take a mugshot of you. You probably put a free one up on Facebook and Instagram.

Your computer, tablet, and smartphone are probably fingerprint-activated as well. Authorities more than likely have your fingerprint, too.

Yes, "social" media does have its benefits. It can be used to promote yourself and your business in a positive light. But if you're in the game and putting up pictures searching for likes, you're making it easier for you to be searched.

Plus, putting pictures up for likes and attention is a cry for something of deeper meaning you may seek in your life. I'm not here to tell you what that thing may be—only your **self**ie can.

To return to my original point, quit playing checkers and hop on the chessboard. Think about your moves because every one of them counts.

Life's Tough, but You Have to Face It!

Life is tough sometimes. Reality can be harsh, but that is no reason not to face it. A lot of us like to drown ourselves in a fantasy world. The funny thing is that a fantasy world can never be more interesting than your real world, but a lot of people think so; that's why they indulge in fantasy football.

With the advent of the 2020 pandemic, every sports institution has been canceled until further notice. If we were to let wisdom whisper in our ears, this shutdown has been a blessing in disguise.

Look at all the things that can be accomplished when our time and energy are directed to the purpose of our own making. What if we learned to put the time and effort that we used on collecting stats and information on other men (because *essentially* that's what it is, keeping tabs on what other men do) and spent that time studying and investing in the stock market?

Or we can use this time to study how to start a business. The pandemic has shown everyone that our jobs can be taken away at a moment's notice. We should think of ways to start businesses and hustles that will bring our family and ourselves additional income. Think of ways never to be caught off guard again.

You may think that fantasy football is just entertainment, and to some, it is, but entertainment has always been used to distract the masses (us) from things that truly matter, like our goals and ambitions.

Living in reality will help us to focus on those things that truly matter. Instead of running from our problems, we now have time to address them. We can learn to heal ourselves mentally and emotionally. This is a time to meditate and study daily.

Clearing our minds will help us live in a real fantasy of our own making. As your mind clears and your goals become near, you will wish you would have begun this journey earlier, but never fret over the past. You only have this moment to make things right.

Reality gets more complicated when you don't face it head-on. We all have to straighten up and quit running from it. The void will only get deeper if we continue to live in a fantasy world.

This book's running theme is to have you break away from all forms of media and tune back into being who you were put here to be, and that's a great person!

Turn Hood Logic into Good Logic!

The mentality in the hood is that everybody is a tough guy. You know that *nobody better test me because I have to prove that I am a tough guy* mentality. That tough mentality has people doing things out of pure emotion and ego, never giving their actions a logical thought beforehand.

I was driving in my old neighborhood when I noticed four young teenage girls walking down the middle of the street. As I got closer, they all did what any thinking person would do and moved to get out of the way of the approaching car. Then, suddenly, one of them was struck with hood logic and decided to walk back into the street as if she was going to test me.

When I saw her grin and look back at my car, I knew what time it was. I kept my pace to see how far she would go, but she smartened up and moved out of the way.

She and her friends laughed, but the laughing ceased when I stopped the car and rolled down my window to say something to her.

I looked at her with a stupid face and said, "Baby girl, pay attention!" I could've and should've said so much more, but it didn't pop into my mind at that moment.

She looked a little embarrassed. It was probably more embarrassing and shocking to her that a handsome male said something to her other than what she was used to. Our teens have gotten used to doing silly things and getting away with them.

That wasn't the first time I had to say something to a young lady for thinking she was the toughest thing moving. The next time, my mom was driving. While we drove down the road, a young lady decided to look at our car, saw that we were coming, but then proceeded to walk in front of us.

After my mom stopped so she didn't hit the girl, I rolled down the window and said, "You're a beautiful young lady with your whole life ahead of you, but you could've ruined it all if we'd hit you. What if the driver didn't care about you and decided to hit you? Then what? You would've been a dead girl in the streets. Baby girl, please use your beautiful brain!"

Living in the hood breeds a mentality of not caring about anything. We all walk around acting like we don't give a flying f***. But it's an act, an act that doesn't give us anything out of life except hurt and destruction.

I know because I bombed my whole first year in college because of hood logic or emotion. That's what it is: an emotion and feeling that clouds our ability to think logically and to see the bigger picture. The two stories above are examples of hood logic that will get us nowhere fast in life.

Logic would tell you that a car is a ton of metal, so if you were to get hit by one, it could kill or severely injure you. And with the number of people texting and driving, who knows if the driver is even paying attention to you or the road.

My brother E. is living with the effects of a person who was driving while texting. He is now missing a leg.

Life isn't a game of Frogger. Life isn't a game at all! Learn to think out all situations to the end. Hood logic has us playing checkers while the rest of the world is playing chess.

Get Out of the Way, Mr. Invincible!

On my way home one night, as I was about to turn onto my street, I heard a loud pop and screech noise out of nowhere. I looked to the left, and a car was flying up the street. It sporadically hit the curb and swerved into the bus stopped at the light.

Since I wasn't trying to get hit, I turned around and jogged back a couple of yards to get out of the way, just in case the car didn't come to a stop.

The car swerved, skidded, and then made an illegal left turn, then a quick right turn down my street. I initially thought this person was running from the cops because I heard sirens in the background.

When I got home, I told my sister about what just happened, and she explained to me how people have died because they thought they were invincible or that nothing out of the ordinary would ever happen to them.

I know a lot of people would have just kept walking as if nothing had happened. Every other day, I see someone walking in front of a moving car like they're Superman as if the car wouldn't hurt them if it hit them. Or I will see someone walk in front of the car with that "they better not hit me" attitude on their face.

That attitude annoys the living daylight out of me because Mr. Invincible doesn't know what kind of day the driver has had. Maybe they just want to kill someone, and you look like an easy target strolling across the street. Mr. Invincible never thinks about how the driver might not even see him because he is driving while looking at his phone. Mr. Invincible never thinks that the brakes on the car might not be in top-notch condition. These things should be accounted for, but they aren't because people think, *Hey, I'm Invincible!*

That Mr. Invincible mentality needs to be thrown out the window. It's time that we all start processing and using our critical thinking skills in our everyday lives. For instance, my sister and I were walking down the same street when we noticed that the wall to the person's house that lives across from the street where the car swerved was destroyed. Someone had run into it with their car. We noticed car parts scattered throughout the whole yard.

Critical thinking made me jog back a couple of yards to a place of safety. I quickly thought about the car doing the same thing as the last car, but this time, it would've crashed into me and the wall. You never know when your last day will be, but why put yourself in unnecessary danger? No one is truly invincible.

ORGANIZATION

To be successful, you must organize everything in your life. If this book hasn't moved you to grab a pen and pad, please do so now, then write a to-do list of everything you need to do to progress to the next level in your life. Once you knock off an item, cross it off the list and move on to the next.

Success doesn't come with luck; it comes with a well-executed plan that lays out all the necessary steps it would take to obtain that success. Success isn't defined only by monetary gains. Success for me means to be completely healthy and strong physically, mentally, and soulfully (spiritually). Your success can only be defined by you!

The reason for so much emphasis on writing out your plan is that you cannot and will not find a Fortune 500 company without a well-written business plan, mission, and vision statement. Your life is a business in the sense that it needs to be run with the same organization and order as a successful business.

You should have a mission and vision statement for the direction of your life. You may be the type of carefree person who goes with the wind. That's fine. Just don't be the person who continues to ask the person who did plan their life out for continuous help. Don't be that guy! Please don't be that guy! The key to your success is write (right) in your hands.

We all have been dealt different hands in life. Please don't think I am one of those silver spoon-fed people trying to feed you a fairy tale. I'm from Wilkinsburg. I won't explain much more about where I'm from, but I will say that I do what I do to uplift my hood and yours. The hood needs to be rebuilt and redefined. It can't and won't be built until we build the hearts and minds of the people who live within it.

That's why I am screaming, "Organization!"

We need organization! It starts with you. Being successful within yourself makes it easier to give a helping hand to the next man as long as the next man is serious about his life and isn't trying to smooch off of you.

Start by organizing the physical clutter of your home. Clutter in the physical highly correlates with clutter in the mind. A clean dwelling place gives your mind more serenity. A peaceful mind is a clear mind. A clear mind is a focused mind.

Once your home is built, you can move on to the next home, and the next home, and the next home. The ripple effect has begun. Your organization has just rebuilt your community.

Digitally Divided Families

Wikipedia defines the Digital Divide as an economic and social inequality regarding access to, use of, or impact of information and communications technology (cell phones, tablets, personal computers, internet, and other electronics).

After reading the chapter about overcoming temptation, you know that most words usually have a double meaning. As you know, most words have a meaning that is derived from something else. The double entendre meaning of the *digital divide* could also mean how everything digital has divided humans from their humanity.

We are losing our ability to interact with one another. I see parents indulging in their phones while their baby cries for attention. We are all guilty of playing on our phones instead of interacting and enjoying the presence of our company. It happens. I'm guilty of it. You're guilty of it. We all are guilty of it. Our attention has been digitally divided.

We need a Digital Subtraction. We all need to reduce our use of electronics drastically. Not only do electronics reduce our mental strength and powers, but they also poison us with their radiation.

Think about it. How many phone numbers do you remember besides your immediate family members?

Not too many these days. I had to memorize a number in my youth, or it was forever lost.

I have learned some things we can do to regain our humanity. The next time you and your family go out to eat, everyone must leave their phone in the car. Sit at the booth or table and have an honest conversation with one another.

You will be surprised at how much you can find out about your family when you sit down and converse with them. Forget about Facebook statuses, Instagram photos, or (I can barely say this word without retching) Tweets. Only focus on what is happening in this present moment with your loved ones.

This is a fun idea to do with your friends on your next outing; everyone must put their phone on silent and place it face down on the table. The first person to touch their phone must pay for everyone's meal. Who wants to come out of their pocket because they can't restrain themselves? Playing mind games with people to get them to pick up their phones is fun. If you try it, watch how much you laugh during your outing.

Those are just two ways to subtract digital interference from our lives. Doing simple things will make family outings so much fun. Families will start to grow together and be close-knit again. We will start to appreciate one another like we used to.

Tight-knit families bring peace to our worlds. A close family also brings unity and peace to the world around us. Hopefully, that last statement makes the following chapter more understandable.

Family Equals Perfection

I can see you reading the title of this chapter and thinking, "Okay, Cliff, you made some valid points thus far, but come on now! Family Equals Perfection? My family is far from perfect! You tried it!" Ha! I feel you because I honestly don't know a perfect family.

Hopefully, this story will help to clarify what I mean.

I was outside hooping with my friend Rob and his dad. It was scorching hot. There were no trees for shade, and the sky was clear without a cloud in sight. The sun was passing down all the sun codes that day.

I was guarding Rob while his dad brought the ball up the court. I looked at Rob's dad, then back at Rob, and then it hit me: they looked **exactly** alike. The revelation was so simple that all I could do was laugh.

The Bible says that we are created in God's image and likeness. We were also given the ability to create in his image. When a man creates a child, the child is made in the image of that man. Most of us can agree that when a child is born, it looks like either the mother or father, right?

Rob's father created Rob in his image. That also means that Rob's grandfather created Rob's father in his image as well. Now think about how far back that goes. It goes back to the beginning of time or man's creation.

If the original man portrayed the image of God onto his kids, and his kids portrayed it onto their kids, and so on, that would mean that the kids of today are still made in God's image and likeness. The image of God is perfection.

We all carry within us every strand of DNA passed down through our ancestry from the beginning of time, but we have forgotten this knowledge and stopped practicing our close-knit family culture.

As parents, we are our children's gods. No child is born with a Bible, Quran, or Metu Neter ingrained in their hands. We are the only people that our children look to every day to provide food, clothes, and shelter. When a child cries and is upset, they look to their parents for all the answers. As parents, we portray the image of God to our children.

We must be careful about how we conduct ourselves around our children. As mentioned in Somebody's Watching, it is a monkey-see, monkey-do world. Your child will emulate what they see you doing. We must lead by example. Don't do things you wouldn't want your child to do. We should strive hard to avoid being "Do as I say, not as I do" parents.

Keeping the family together can be challenging because we make choices, and sometimes, those choices lead to having a child with someone we didn't see a future with. But to my queens with baby fathers that they can't stand, I'm sorry that you are in that situation, but you have to do everything possible to keep that child's father in his kid's life as long as he isn't detrimental to your child's well-being.

Having a father or a father figure around will make a significant difference in your child's life. Looking back at my life, I am thankful that I was blessed enough to grow up with my dad in the household. It allowed me to see how a man should and shouldn't interact with a woman.

My dad also taught me things that my mom wouldn't have been able to. Plus, boys tend to fear men more than women, making the man a stronger authoritative figure in the eyes of a young male.

When the family structure is strong, years and years of knowledge and wisdom will be passed down through every generation, making the next generation stronger than the last. Our goal is to make our children better than we are, and then when they have children, we pray they do the same thing. Perfection will be on the horizon with every generation as the family continues to improve.

Family, I end this book with the hope that something within it touches you and inspires you to take the necessary steps to enhance your life and those around you.

Strong families are the key to our power. Family protects you from the world. Much more can be written about the importance of family. I will write more about family in my next book, but I will leave it here to keep this book 100. I pray that you and your family live lives filled with Love, Joy, Peace, Power, and Prosperity!

Thank You!

Thank you for purchasing and reading Less Than a Sack of Weed. If this book has positively moved you, would you do me a favor and write a review? Your review will help this book reach more people.

Let's stay connected:

@cliffgr33n on all social media
&
Go to **www.cliffgr33n.com** to stay up to date on future projects.

Spread Love & Share Wisdom!